Phil 4:11-13

The
Success
Puzzle

Dick Kelsey

CROSSBOOKS
PUBLISHING

CrossBooks™
A Division of LifeWay
1663 Liberty Drive
Bloomington, IN 47403
www.crossbooks.com
Phone: 1-866-879-0502

First published by CrossBooks 3/18/2013

ISBN: 978-1-4627-2604-2 (sc)
ISBN: 978-1-4627-2605-9 (e)

Library of Congress Control Number: 2013904108

The Success Puzzle, Dick Kelsey, P.O. Box 464, Eureka Springs, Arkansas 72756

Printed in the United States of America

This book is printed on acid-free paper.

TABLE OF CONTENTS

INTRODUCTION

Succeeding in life is like a puzzle. To achieve success, there are a number of principles, or puzzle pieces, that need to fit together. These pieces, when brought together, will complete the puzzle and lead you to your goal. In this book I try to give a short summary of these pieces. When they fit together you can have the type of life God wants for you. You can enjoy a life of fulfillment and success or as Jesus said in Luke 2:52, "life more abundantly."

Thirty four years ago, when I was 32, I wrote a book called *Winning Ways – Principles of Success for Christian Teens*. I sold 5,000 books in one year. At the time I was the administrator of a Christian school I had co-founded. I taught a Bible class and a government class. In the Bible class I developed a series of lessons about the basic principles of success in life as seen in the scripture.

I was exposed to these principles of success as a 17 year old who, while still in high school, left a secure job at a florist that I enjoyed to sell Fuller Brush door-to-door. Some people laughed at me and thought I was crazy, but I laughed all the way to the bank. While doing this work, and as a salesman for a Bible publishing company, I attended many "success motivation" meetings and seminars.

At each of these seminars and meetings I heard similar ideas. We need to have a positive attitude, work hard, set goals, be persistent, etc. The material was primarily rooted in the research and books by Napoleon Hill, often referred to as the "father of motivational material." He studied the lives of the most successful people of his time, such people as Henry Ford, Thomas Edison, President Theodore Roosevelt, and Alexander Graham Bell plus a hundred others. He found that all of these people seemed to apply certain principles in their lives. Hill shared this research in books such as *Think and Grow Rich*, *The Law of Success*, *Science of Success* and others.

As I learned these principles and tried to apply them to my life, I recognized that all of these ideas come right from the scripture. As Solomon wrote in Ecclesiastes 1:9, "… and there is nothing new under the sun." These principles of success go back thousands of years and are seen throughout the entire Bible.

My goal in rewriting this book of 34 years ago is to share from a personal stand point how it worked out in my life. I do so with the hope that other people like me, can enjoy a fruitful and fulfilling life. That is what God wants for all of us, and I hope that you pick up a few ideas that move you in that direction.

CHAPTER 1
HOW IT STARTED

On Christmas Day, 1950, all eight of the Kelsey children gathered around the Christmas tree with our mother and father opening each gift one at a time – a Kelsey tradition.

Christmas Morning 1950
*Dick Kelsey is the youngest next to the tree
in the middle of the picture.*

We ranged in age from me, who would turn four the next week, to my brother Roy who was twenty-three. Little did we realize that in 16 days all of our lives would change forever. On the morning of January 10, 1951, my father went to the doctor's office in the local hospital to get a note to clear him to go back to work after being off for a week because of illness. At the hospital, he died suddenly of a heart attack in the rest room. No one in the family was aware of previous heart issues.

With five children still at home, my mother, whose education went to the 8th grade, had the challenge of keeping the family together. My father served in World War I and worked at the ship yard in Philadelphia under civil service. Thus my mother was entitled to a small pension from each of these systems. The military pension was for each child until they were eighteen. We lived in the house my father had built and which, fortunately, was paid for. In the 1950's, there were no food stamps, medical care, help with heating costs, or other such programs for families like ours. You had to make it on your own.

I learned at a very early age that money didn't grow on trees or in my mom's purse. If I wanted something I had to earn the money to pay for it myself. I started collecting empty pop bottles to redeem for two cents each, collecting old newspapers and shoveling snow. By the time I was eight years old I had saved enough so I could buy my own suit to wear to church. In that day even young boys wore suits and ties to church – sounds weird doesn't it? I was very proud of that suit!

"Dick Kelsey in his first suit."

By the time I was twelve, I had a newspaper route serving 150 afternoon customers a day, six days a week. I also developed a lawn mowing business mowing grass for 25 regular customers. I was able to buy my first boat, which I used on Woodbury Creek, that took me onto the Delaware River across from Philadelphia.

When I was old enough to take a "real job" I went to work for Sweeten Brothers Florists.

That was a family business owned by men who were active in our local church. Most of my brothers started working, outside the home, as employees of Sweeten Brother Florists. During the summer I would work in the green houses changing dirt in the flower beds (a very hot, sweaty job) working six eight-hour days for a dollar an hour. That was the minimum wage at the time. I remember getting my pay envelope with $48 cash in it. I was in the big time!

At seventeen, someone talked to me about getting into direct selling with the Fuller Brush Company. I went door- to-door selling hair brushes, mops, brooms, etc. I took the orders and delivered them a week later. Working after school and on

Saturdays, I was able to double my previous income and more. In that day, door-to-door sales were easier, since most women were stay-at-home moms.

While working for the Fuller Brush Company, I attended my first motivational seminar. Speakers would share how we could become a much more successful salesman and try to inspire us to set and reach higher goals in your work. I was captivated. I learned that there were certain basic principles in life that, if followed, would make one successful.

At Bible College in Fort Wayne, Indiana, I was recruited by another student to spend the summer after my freshman year selling Bibles for South Western Publishing Company. It too was door- to door- selling. I worked 80 hours per week for ten weeks selling Nave's Topical Bible. I still use one of those Bibles. I made more money in ten weeks than most of my peers made in a year. Since I was paying my own way through college, this helped a lot. There were no Pell Grants back then. The second summer, I sold Bibles and was a sales manager with sixteen people working for me. I managed and sold as well. Again, it was very good money. I was able to purchase a brand new Pontiac Lemans.

If someone worked for South Western Publishing Company, They had to attend one week of training in Tennessee at their own expense. They taught me to sell the books and Bibles I carried. They also had many sessions with some of the most famous motivational speakers of the time. These talks were very inspiring. I also began to realize their basic message came back to the same essential principles that Napoleon Hill had set forth in his works fifty years before. Principles the Bible set forth thousands of years before.

I cannot conclude this chapter about my beginning years without sharing what I believe to be one of the most important influences on my growing up years. When my father was living, he took all of us to our local church, the First Baptist Church of Woodbury, New Jersey. After he passed away, we continued to go Sunday morning and night and Wednesday evening. As a youth I was active in our youth group. The thing I remember most about my church involvement, aside from my decision to accept Christ as my Savior, was the support the church gave to me as an individual. Our Sunday school class did things together, and our teacher took us boys camping and on other activities I wouldn't have had the opportunity to do without my church involvement. I can remember various men in the church rubbing my head and telling me, "Richard, you're going to do all right." They helped me believe in myself. I lived in a single-parent home, but the advantage I had was that the people in the church helped make up for what I was missing. This should be a ministry of every church. Give extra attention to kids from single-parent homes.

As a teenager, I made a decision that affected me for the rest of my life. At youth camp I was challenged by a sermon about Matthew 6:33. In that verse we are told by Jesus to "… seek first the kingdom of God and His righteousness, and all these things shall be added unto you." I like making money. I was good at it. But I determined then that making money would not be the focal point of what I did. I committed my life to Ministry, which often did not pay much. I graduated from four years of Bible College. A small church called me to be their pastor for which I was paid $75 per week – with no benefits except the parsonage. However throughout the years I always had opportunities to earn extra money to provide for my family and have a few "extra" things. Even at the age of forty, I still had no real net worth. But God's promise held true and as the years rolled on, God has blessed financially in a way that I could have never imagined.

CHAPTER 2
WHAT'S IT ALL ABOUT

B efore I begin a discussion about the various principles that enable a person to be successful in life, I want to take a few moments to give a definition of success. What is it?

Many people equate success with money, fame, power or some other spectacular achievement. A professional football player wants to help win the Super Bowl. A professional baseball player wants to contribute to a World Series victory for his team. A politician may want to be the governor or even president. These things are fine but do not constitute genuine success. You can be rich and miserable, powerful and a poor leader.

Real success from a biblical stand-point is defined as fulfilling God's plan for your life. God put all of us on this earth for a reason. We are not accidents, even though our parents may have referred to us as one. When my father found out I was coming along when he was 48 years old, he probably thought he was accident prone!

To achieve true success, we must be doing God's will for our lives. Sure, we can be relatively happy doing what we think we want to do and we might even make a little money doing it. But when we realize that our truest and deepest desires are, in fact, the will of God for our lives, we will be successful and truly happy.

When I was in my middle and later teens, I was confronted with a very basic decision about my life. A number of well meaning people were urging me to go into business. I had proven I knew how to earn money and they believed I could have a very successful business career. I had been challenged at camp and in youth meetings to go into the ministry. The turning point verse for me was Matthew 6:33 (which I referred to in the previous chapter) where Jesus states in the Sermon On The Mount, "But seek first the kingdom of God and His righteousness, and all these things shall be added unto you." Now that I have lived a good bit of my life, I can see, looking back, God's fulfillment of this verse in my life. I spent many years in full-time ministry and my entire life helping others. I have in my later years realized God's abundant blessing in the financial and material aspect of life. My wife and I live well and have been blessed with much.

How do we know God's will for our lives? I could spend many pages discussing this but let me summarize with the following points. To know God's will for our lives, we must first know God in a personal way. We need to have come to the place where we recognize our personal sinfulness, recognize that Jesus Christ died for us, and by faith receive Jesus Christ into our lives. Read the third chapter of John for further information.

Be open to God's will. You cannot decide what you want to do and then ask God if that is okay. Read God's Word. As you read the Bible, you get to know God better and can begin to understand His will for our life.

Talk to others. Find out how God directed them into the work they are doing. In Proverbs, Solomon writes, "in the multitude of counselors there is wisdom". Other people can give you various things you should think about as you look at ideas of what God might want for your life.

Remember, God will give you the ability and resources you need to do His will. Don't limit your thinking to what you can do on your own, but recognize that God's resources are limitless.

Start moving in some directions. It is easier to direct a car, boat, or plane that is moving much easier than one that is sitting still.

The first chapter of Psalms begins with the phrase, "Blessed is the man…" and then in verse three states, "… whatsoever he does shall prosper." God wants to bless your life, but you can only really experience God's blessing when you are living according to His will.

Quotes:

"Whatever is at the center of our lives will be the source of our security, guidance, wisdom, and power." Stephen Covey.

"If I have been of service, if I have glimpsed more of the nature and essence of ultimate good, if I am inspired to reach wider horizons of thought and action, if I am at peace with myself, it has been a successful day." Alex Noble

"The starting point of all achievement is desire." Napoleon Hill

"Happiness lies in the joy of achievement and the thrill of creative effort." Franklin D. Roosevelt

"Success comes from knowing that you did your best to become the best that you are capable of becoming." John Wooden

"Strive not to be a success, but rather to be of value." Albert Einstein

"Success is getting what you want. Happiness is wanting what you get." Dale Carnegie

CHAPTER 3

THINKING RIGHT – DEVELOPING PMA

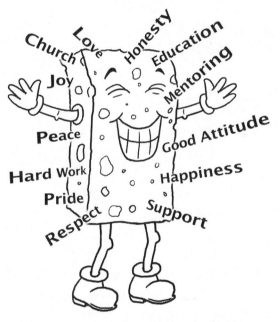

Church Love Honesty Education Mentoring

Joy

Peace Good Attitude

Hard Work Happiness

Pride

Respect Support

"Soak up positive thoughts and you will have positive actions."

We must learn to develop and maintain a positive mental attitude. Our attitude is how we think, not how we feel. Feelings are usually based on emotions. Attitude is based on us deciding how we will think.

Some people are by nature more positive than negative in their attitudes. Others tend to always see the dark side of things. Since all of us have a sin nature, we are all drawn toward the negative and must make an effort to be positive. If you disagree with this statement think, for a minute about what happens if I say ten good things about a person and one negative thing. What will most people repeat? What will be most remembered? The negative item will be remembered and repeated. People complain that news is all negative. The problem is negative news is what people want to know about. People claim not to like negative political campaigns, but candidates use them. Why? Because they work. If a candidate for office runs a positive campaign, and his or her opponent runs a negative attack campaign, the negative campaign generally wins. That is because people usually believe the negative information even, when it is not true.

The Apostle Paul was positive, even in the worst of circumstances. From prison he wrote Philippians chapter 4, which I call the "Positive Mental Attitude" chapter of the Bible. In verse 4 of that chapter we are told to, "Rejoice in the Lord always …" In verse 6 he tells us, "Be anxious for nothing …" In verse 8 he tells us to think on what is good, true, lovely, etc. In verse 11 he relates how he has learned "… in whatever state I am, to be content." Finally, Paul caps it off in verse 13 by saying from prison, "I can do all things through Christ who strengthens me." I don't know about you, but to me that is all some real positive thinking.

In order to develop a positive mental attitude, we need to first learn how our mind works. Our brain is like a super computer. No computer, no matter how huge, touches the magnificence of our brain. Psychologists tell us our brain is divided into the subconscious and the conscious. There is the subconscious and the conscious. The subconscious stores information. Everything you and I ever hear, say, see, experience, and read becomes a permanent part of our subconscious mind. It is always there. Our conscious mind makes decisions. Every day all of us make hundreds of decisions based on the information stored in our subconscious.

What we like to eat, what we like to wear, the cars we drive, the movies we watch, are all decided by the information we have stored. The reason some people go into a building and shoot others is they have allowed hatred, bitterness and negative ideas to build up and fester until they end up making terrible decisions. No computer can produce anything unless basic information was put into the programming first. If our computer is filled with garbage, negative things, then we will get negative thinking out which result in negative actions.

Our mind is the one thing that God has given us total control over. Senator John McCain survived over six years of torture in a Hanoi prison because he determined never to let his captors control his mind. People who are successful in sports, business, and all walks of life are people who have learned to control their attitudes. They do not let someone else who is having a bad day ruin their day.

How do we develop a Positive Mental Attitude?

I would like to make three suggestions:

First, begin by putting positive things into your mind. Remember, everything you see, hear, read, experience become part of your subconscious. Read positive material, or watch movies that have a positive message. Realize that negative input will lead to negative conscious decisions. This is why reading God's word is so important. Keep in mind Philippians 4:8. "Finally brethren, whatever things are true, whatever things are noble, whatever things are lovely, whatever things are just, whatever things are pure, whatever things are lovely whatever things are of good report, if there is any virtue and if there is anything praiseworthy, meditate on these things." The verb for meditate in the original Greek means "to continue to think on, ponder. It is a present continuous verb that means we keep on thinking on these positive things.

Second it is very important who we hang around with. I have said in hundreds of lessons and talks on this subject, "We become like those we are around." Eventually we become like the people we associate with. We talk like them, think like them and act like them. We hang around negative people and you will become a negative person. Hang around positive people and you will become a positive person. For ten years I owned and operated a residential boys' home for juvenile offenders. In visiting with the boys one by one, so many of them shared that the court took them out of their home and put them in our facility because of what they did while with other kids. I cannot remember a boy who got in trouble by himself. Someone else got them to drink that beer or use those drugs or steal a car. Successful people associate with successful people. When I was in ninth grade, my algebra teacher taught the class to play chess. He believed it did the same good for us as algebra. It made us think. He told us to always try and play chess with someone who was better than we were. That is how a person learns to grow and get better in chess. That is also how we learn to grow and improve in life – be with people who are stronger than we are.

Take action. Positive action leads to positive attitudes. In my direct selling days I remember being told to walk fast to the door because that will help you have a positive attitude at the door. One speaker claimed that successful people walk twenty-five percent faster than the average person. For years people would ask why I walked so fast. When we are faced with a project, it is easy to sit around and think about it. If we think long enough we can think of many reasons why we should not take on the project. But if we take action it will positively affect us and before long we are proud of our accomplishment.

In 1990 I was helping The Church of God of Kansas sell a 127 acre campground the denomination owned by Lake Afton in Goddard, Kansas. We had a potential sale, but problems developed and the deal fell through. In that process, I had become very familiar with the property. It had been losing large sums of money for a number of years and was in serious disrepair. I also saw what I believed was positive potential. I met with the leader of the organization and made a proposal to buy it myself. Since I had no money, I needed them to carry the loan for a period of time until the campground became profitable. We were able to come together with a deal that was good for both of us. For deals to work, they must benefit both sides.

When I mentioned to some of my pastor friends that I was buying the campground, one pastor from a large church, who was a good friend, told me, "Dick, if you buy that you will go broke!" Since I was already broke, I thought that didn't matter. I looked at the opportunity through positive glasses. He was looking at it through negative glasses. I did lose money for the first few years, and in fact took no income for myself during that time. By maintaining a positive attitude toward my original vision, and with a lot of hard work by my entire family, we were able to make a successful operation out of that campground. In three years we were able to get a bank loan to pay off the Church of God, build some new buildings and improve the property and operation. When I look back, having a positive attitude toward that project, instead of listening to negative naysayers, changed my life.

You can have a positive mental attitude. You just have to decide you are going to be positive and then do it. Before long it will become a habit and take you far down the road to a successful and productive life.

Quotes:

"Our attitude determines our altitude." Zig Ziglar

"Some of us need a check up from the neck up." Zig Ziglar

"A positive mind finds a way it can be done, a negative mind looks for all the ways it can't be done." Napoleon Hill

"They succeed, because they think they can." Virgil

"Belief in oneself is one of the important bricks in building any successful venture." Lydia M. Child

"In order to succeed, your desire for success should be greater than your fear of failure." Bill Cosby

"In order to succeed, we must first believe that we can." Nikos Kazantzakis

"The more man meditates upon good thoughts, the better will be his world and the world at large." Confucius

CHAPTER 4
ON TARGET – PRINCIPLES
OF GOAL SETTING

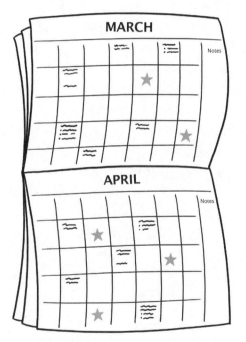

"Set clear goals with specific dates for completion."

A man walks into a travel agency and says, "I would like to buy a ticket please." The ticket agent naturally responds with, "Where would you like to go?" To fly somewhere, you must first know where you are going. Many people act just like the destination-less man. To do something worthwhile for God and others, you must first know where you are going and why. It is important that each of us know how to set goals and then reach them.

There are two types of goals:

1. **Long Range Goals.** These are goals that you have for your life, for a few years, a year, or even for a period of months. What do you want to do with your life? What kind of work do you want to do? What kind of occupation can you get into where you are doing what you love, so you do not dread going to work but look forward to it every day. Long range goals can be made in different areas of your life. Family, your Christian involvement, work, education, plus others can all have separate long range goals. If you set no long range goals, you will drift in life and never get where you really want to be or accomplish what you really want to achieve.

2. **Short Range Goals.** This is where we take our long range goals and break them down into smaller segments. If you want a college degree, how do you achieve the first year of getting that degree? If you want to save a large sum of money, how much do you need to save each week or month? If you want to lose weight, what is your goal for each week or month? Breaking long range goals down into manageable segments is vitally important.

"Learn to set your goals high and eventually
you will grow into them"

Over the years whether it was as a pastor of a church, running a Christian school, or operating a business, each year, usually in January, I would meet with staff and set out our goals for the coming year. What improvements would we make? How could we grow and expand? How could all of us personally grow in our own lives and abilities? We would write our thoughts down and then throughout the year we would bring them out to see how we were doing. This helped us stay focused on our goals for the organization and on our goals for ourselves.

Writing out both your long range and short range goals is very important. It is too easy for goals to become vague or fussy. By writing goals out on paper you are able to make them more specific and clear. It helps with some goals if you put them on a small card and tape them to your bathroom mirror. This way you are reminded each day what a given goal is.

Having been involved in many businesses, I have written many business plans. A business plan is essentially a set of goals that give your business direction. A good plan for a new start up business will include:

A. Who you are and what your over-all mission is. (Not just making money.)

B. What the total investment will be in order to get started and maintain the business for at least one year. Most new businesses fail because of lack of initial capital.

C. What is the worst thing that could happen if this business were to fail?

D. What is the best case of what would happen if the business succeeds?

E. What is the most likely outcome?

To start a business without a written business plan that has been reviewed by others who are in business would be foolish. To start a day without goals for the day is also a mistake. I usually make a list each day of what I hope to accomplish that day. It brings great satisfaction when you actually complete your list for that day.

Goals are important for two reasons:

1. Goals give direction. With clear goals, you know where you are going. Always remember that if you aim at nothing, you will usually hit nothing. Goals help you to set priorities. What is most important to you today, this week, this month, this year? None of us can do everything we want to do. We usually would not have the resources or the time. We need to decide what is most important and set priorities.

2. They provide motivation. All of us need motivation. Motivation is what gets us going and keeps us going. Some motivation is provided by need. We are hungry and we need money to buy food. The greater motivation is when we have a vision, a goal in mind that we are striving to achieve. That will keep us going when the going gets tough.

The man who actually knows just what he wants in life has already gone a long way toward attaining it. We accomplish very little in life without goals.

Quotes:

"Definiteness of purpose is the starting point of all achievement."
W. Clement Stone

"One may miss the mark by aiming too high as too low." Thomas Fuller

"Setting goals is the first step in turning the invisible into the visible." Tony Robbins

"What you get by achieving your goals is not as important as what you become by achieving your goals." Henry David Thoreau

"Set your goals high, and don't stop till you get there." Bo Jackson

CHAPTER 5
WORK – IT'S GREAT!

All of us have lessons in life that we learned from the home and environment in which we were raised. The Kelsey kids of Woodbury, of whom I was the youngest, benefited greatly from the work ethic example of our father. Our Dad worked hard to provide for his family and worked hard for others. He often helped others with jobs and would accept no pay for his work even though he could have used the money. I began working and earning money when I was eight years old, helping to buy my own clothes and getting the things I wanted, such as pop and candy. During my teen years I considered work a natural part of life and didn't even give it a second thought. I looked at work as being a great opportunity. I learned well that there is work we do around the house because we are part of the family and we carry our weight. No one in our family ever heard of an allowance. We helped out with household chores because we lived there and enjoyed the benefits of living there such as food and the comforts of a home.

In the principles of success, there is no substitute for work. In some segments of our society, people promote the idea that we should be able to do less and less work and get paid more and more for doing it. This is not a success mentality. A success mentality concerning work is that we should work harder and smarter without thought of what we will get out of it, and then it is returned to us many times over.

The book of Proverbs has many verses concerning the value of work. In Proverbs 10:4 Solomon writes, "Lazy men are soon poor, hard workers get rich." (Living Bible) In 20:13 he writes, "If you love sleep, you will end in poverty. Stay awake, work hard, and there will be plenty to eat." The Apostle Paul writes in 2 Thessalonians 3:10, "…that if any would not work they should not eat." Many young people would get pretty hungry if this verse were applied in their home.

Some people say, "I would like to work, but I can't find a job." My response to that is this: make your own job. Almost anyone can walk around their own neighborhood and find work that needs to be done. Someone needs a yard cleaned, a house painted, a lawn mowed or windows cleaned. If you offer to do the work, most people will pay you to do it. If it is an elderly person who is incapable of doing the work themselves and can't pay, do it anyway. God has a way of returning blessings we give to others. Studies have shown that people who are unemployed for an extended period of time benefit greatly by volunteering for various causes. The involvement with other people and the sense of accomplishment is very helpful in keeping one's spirits up. It can also lead to contacts for a job that someone heard was opening. This exact thing happened with a number of people I know.

Four suggestions to make your work enjoyable:

1. **Learn to look at your work as a challenge**. Whether it is a task at your employment that may be considered

"boring" or a chore at home, look at it as a challenge. How can you do the job better? How can you do it faster? Are there new ways to do this job? In making a job a challenge, be sure you know what the ultimate goal is. What is success in that task?

2. **Plan your work and then work your plan.** A poor plan is better than no plan. What are the tools you will need? Will you need help? Where is the best place to start? If you are painting a room, what do you need to do, first, second, third, etc? Most likely you will need to remove or cover the furniture in the room. You may need to prepare the walls by fixing cracks, holes and such. Then you need the right brushes, rollers or paint sprayer. Follow your plan step by step. Before long you will have achieved success at the task. Many people get frustrated trying to do a job because they are not sure where to start or the best way to proceed. Make a plan and then follow it.

3. **Put your heart and soul into your work.** It will bring you a great sense of satisfaction upon completion. Solomon writes in Ecclesiastes 9:10, "Whatever your hand finds to do, do with all your might." A job that is done half-heartedly will take you twice as long and will provide you with little joy upon completion. When people work hard all day, they may come home tired, but they come home feeling good about themselves and what they accomplished that day. A person who stared at the ceiling most of the day and did little will also come home tired and will not have a sense of accomplishment or satisfaction. Employees at a business are much happier when busy doing useful things than when sitting around watching the clock move slowly from hour to hour. Employers should make sure the people who work for

them are engaged in useful, important work that keeps them busy.

4. **When you complete your work, reward yourself.** If you are working a job for money, the reward comes when you receive your paycheck. If you follow the principles set out in the previous points, that paycheck will grow, or someone else will notice your work and you will get a promotion or a better job. If it is a task at home, reward yourself after completing the job. Take a swim or do something you enjoy after the job is complete.

In concluding this chapter, I want to comment about the difference between working hard, which we all should do, and being a workaholic. A workaholic is a person who works to the point of neglecting their family, their church, or even themselves. Our bodies are not designed to work seven days a week, 18 hours a day, week in and week out. We will quickly burn out. Balance is the key. Time with family and friends is essential. Vacations can recharge your batteries. When you start a business, no doubt you will have to work some long hours. Some businesses are seasonal, requiring hard work for a few months. For years at the campground, I worked very long hours seven days a week for a good part of the summer. It was the nature of the business. At the end of the season I took time off, took a trip, and did something different and enjoyable.

Quotes:

"Success is dependent on effort." Sophacles

"Well done is better than well said." Benjamin Franklin

CHAPTER 6
GETTING OUT IN FRONT BY SHOWING INITIATIVE

"To stand out from the crowd, take the initiative."

If you examine the lives of leaders and successful people, one thing characterizes them all: Initiative. So what is initiative? Webster defines initiative as a noun meaning: 1. The action of taking the first step or move; 2. Ability in originating new ideas or methods.

I like to define initiative as "doing what needs to be done without being told." A successful person, or one who stands out in a crowd, sees a job that needs to be done, then does it. I have given many seminars to both young people and adults on how to start and run a new business. The key to starting a business is to find a need and then fill it. There are all kinds of needs around us all the time, we have to find a way to meet a need and turn a profit doing so.

I have employed hundreds of people over my years in various businesses. Many young people have worked for me. The ones who did well, not only for my company but for themselves, are the ones who learned to see a need and take care of it without having to be told. No employer likes an employee who must constantly be told every little thing to do. In the late 1800's and early 1900's, Andrew Carnegie built a fortune developing the steel industry in our country. He used his fortune to build libraries around the country, some of which are still in use over a hundred years later. He made the statement, "there are two types of men who never amount to anything. One is the fellow who never does anything except that which he is told to do. The other is the fellow who cannot do even that which he is told to do. The man who gets ahead," Carnegie continued, "does the thing that should be done without being told to do it."

As a teenager growing up in southern New Jersey, I worked in a florist shop. Most of the teenage boys who worked there during the summer spent their time in the greenhouses hauling dirt, pulling weeds, and doing other jobs that would be considered dirty, hard, sweaty work. I spent many hot, muggy days working in the greenhouses. While working there, I took every opportunity to learn how to arrange flowers. I would stay after work and get some old flowers from the trash and make up an arrangement to try and learn the basics of flower arranging. One day the boss needed someone up in the front of the shop, in a nice air-conditioned work area, to arrange flowers. He knew I had been working and trying to learn how to arrange flowers. Out of the six to eight boys working in the greenhouses hauling dirt, I was the one called upon to go up front to the air conditioned work area. Before long, I spent most of my time up front while my peers were still in the hot greenhouses hauling dirt. I would not have been given the better job had I not taken the initiative to learn to arrange flowers. I can still make respectable flower arrangements over 50 years later.

Four Things You can Do to Develop Initiative:

1. **Look for things that need to be done.** No matter where you are or what you are doing, there are always additional things that can be done to improve the situation or to better your environment. No employer is going to object if you do extra clean-up. They will appreciate it when you give extra help to a customer. New ideas for doing your job that are significant ought to be discussed with your boss before taking significant initiative. By having that discussion you will still get the credit for showing initiative and your boss will appreciate being consulted. If you make a big change in how you do your job without telling your boss, you may find yourself in hot water because the company might have a good reason for doing the job the way they do.

2. **Learn to ask for additional responsibilities.** If you become more efficient at your present job, approach your boss with the idea that you can do something else in addition to your current responsibilities. Every teacher is impressed with the student who asks for extra work to improve a grade or to increase knowledge in a given area. If you own the company, to grow and prosper you will always have to look for better ways of serving your customers. If you don't, someone else will!

3. **Strive to become knowledgeable in new areas with which you are not familiar.** Never in the history of mankind has knowledge been so available. The internet has made information so available, most of the time at no cost, that we can learn new things each day and hardly ever scratch the surface. Classes at nearby colleges are available to help improve your knowledge of a given area or to develop new areas of expertise. We must always keep in mind that many employers pay the most for what we know, not how well we do the same thing over and over. The greater your knowledge, the greater your paycheck.

4. **Welcome new challenges.** When you are asked to do something new that you have never done before, don't be apprehensive and think, "I can't do that." Instead think, "I can and I will do it," and then do your best. It is important to acknowledge to your boss that a task is new to you. Assure him or her that you will work hard and do the best you can. I have had people work for me who always claimed they could do things they couldn't. It did not take long to discover they were bluffing. It would have been much better if they had acknowledged that this was something they had never done before but they were glad to try. Then I could have given them the help they needed to succeed instead of spending more time and money fixing their mess.

If you learn to take initiative, before long you will stand out from the rest of the crowd. You will find yourself doing things you never dreamed you'd be able to do. People will ask you to take on additional responsibilities. These opportunities may include a raise. Many doors of opportunity will open to you because people have noticed that you are a man or woman who can see what needs to be done and do it without being told.

Quotes:

"The right man is the one who seizes the moment." Johann Wolfgang von Goethe

"A man who has to be convinced to act before he acts is not a man of action. You must act as you breathe." Georges Clemmenceau

"Even if you're on the right track, you'll get run over if you sit there." Will Rogers

"I couldn't wait for success, so I went ahead without it." Jonathan Winters

CHAPTER 7
BOSSING YOURSELF:
EXERCISING SELF-DISCIPLINE

The word discipline often has a negative connotation. If you are disciplined, punished for doing something wrong, it's not a pleasant experience. This is what I called imposed discipline, somebody else making you do what you ought to do.

There is another type of discipline that is far better – self-discipline. I define self-discipline as doing what you ought to do when you ought to do it. It is being your own boss.

Napoleon Hill, often referred to as the father of modern motivational material, declares in his study course *Science of Success*, "The matter of self-discipline is one of the greatest of all essentials for success. Indeed, if one cannot master himself, he has little hope of mastering anything or anyone else."

No athlete has ever becomes a good athlete unless he learns to develop self-discipline. One must train, practice, and work out in order to succeed in sports. In our spiritual lives, self-discipline is necessary to grow in spiritual perspective. We must read the Bible, pray, meet with other believers on a regular basis, and then use the gifts God has given us if we are going to grow spiritually.

Too many times we live by our feelings and not by doing what we ought to do when we ought to do it. Imagine if you went to work "when you felt like it." You probably wouldn't keep your job very long. Dieting is a form of self-discipline. See-food diets, in which you see the food and thus eat it, won't do much for the waist line. We must determine to exercise self-discipline and eat fewer calories than we burn if we are going to lose any weight. One of the big challenges in the area of losing weight is having the self-discipline long term to keep it off. I have lost the same fifteen pounds a dozen times.

Ways to Develop Self Discipline:

1. **Decide what is really important to you.** Sort out your priorities. The real test of self-discipline comes when a person denies the opportunity to do something he enjoys while pursuing the tasks necessary to bring about his ultimate goals. You need to decide what is most important to you and then set out to do it. When you start a new business you will have to work long hours. You may have to give up some things you like, such as golfing, watching sports on TV, or other fun things while you are getting the business off the ground. Few successful businesses were started without sacrifice and self-discipline on the part of the founder(s).

2. **Consider commitments to yourself as important as commitments made to others.** Many of us do a good job keeping our word to others, but not so well when it comes to commitments we make to ourselves. We think no one is there to notice if we don't follow through on

a commitment we made to ourselves. That is why it is very helpful to have an accountability partner, and why some people do much better in weight loss programs that involve "weighing in" once a week. I know for myself that weighing in has been helpful in keeping me focused. I don't want to have to explain why I gained weight instead of losing it.

3. **Tackle jobs you may not like first**. If you are in college, study for the course you like least before studying for the others. We all like to put off unpleasant tasks to last. Make them first on the list and the rest of the list becomes easier.

4. **Live by principle and not by convenience.** A principle is a truth or an idea we strive to live by. If you are working to reduce your debt, you must exercise self discipline in not spending money for things you don't really need, instead of spending money you don't have just because your credit card will allow it. Most people who are in financial trouble are in trouble because they do not exercise self-discipline in the area of their finances.

Self-discipline is a matter of adopting constructive habits. We are all creatures of habit. Our life is a series of good habits or bad habits. It takes a great deal of self-discipline to develop good habits. Getting up at the same time each day and going to bed about the same time each night is a good habit. It is good for our bodies and helps us to be much more successful. People who use foul language do so as a matter of habit. Our eating patterns are habits. I love ice cream. For years I had a bowl of ice cream each evening. As my weight control became more of an issue, I had to give up that habit. I found it helps a lot if you don't even have it in the house.

Exercising self discipline will free you to do those things you really want to do. It will enable you to achieve the important goals you have set for yourself. Your life becomes much more useful and productive.

CHAPTER 8
DEVELOPING PERSISTENCE

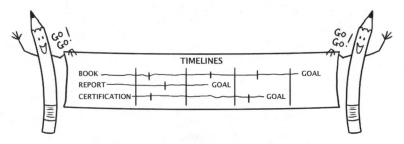

"Don't quit until you reach your goal."

As we move along life's path seeking to achieve our goals, it is very easy to want to quit a project before it comes to a successful conclusion. An important piece of the success puzzle is to be persistent – don't quit. To persist is defined, "to continue steadily or firmly in some state, purpose, or course of action." Another way to say it is "hanging in there."

No one who has truly experienced any degree of success in life, no matter what the field, has done so easily. Nothing worthwhile is accomplished without hard work and persistence. Every successful person has had to learn to continue on in spite of obstacles. Thomas Edison failed over a thousand times before he successfully found and put together the right ideas on how to develop the electric light bulb. The path to his other inventions was strewn with failures, but he persisted and achieved great success with many inventions that have made our lives today more enjoyable and convenient.

"Don't be afraid to stick your neck out"

Throughout my years of starting businesses, running for office and leading organizations, I have experienced many failures. At times I lost large sums of money. I lost elections that I worked hard to win. When I turned our campground into a residential home for troubled youth, I had a tough start. Taking care of kids with five different government agencies regulating you is complicated and difficult. Staff need to be trained, rules followed, forms to filled out. It is easy to mess up especially when your residents are so willing to help you! During the first year I was told by a few people that I should give it up. I didn't. As a result, we helped hundreds of boys over the next ten years before we sold the company to a national organization. During the years I owned and operated the boys' home, I taught a daily class sharing the principles in this book with our residents. One phrase I tried to drill home was, "How does a person go about developing persistence?" Following are a few ideas:

"When the going gets tough, the tough get going. Don't quit."

1. **Get a clear view of your final goal and determine that you will reach it.**
   Too often a person will quit because he does not have a clear concept of what he is trying to do. His goals are vague. Know exactly what you are trying to do, and then make a determination in your heart that you are going to do it, come what may. If you want to be a star basketball player, picture in your mind people cheering as you score

those winning points in a close basketball game. Get the picture clearly in your mind and then determine that you are going to practice regularly, work out, and do everything necessary to become that star player. If starting your own business is your goal, see that business in your mind, determine what it will take to succeed, then stick with it until you do.

2. **Break your goals into segments and then attack each segment until successful.**

There are many steps to go through in starting a business. You need an idea – find a need and then fill it. You need a business plan – how you will go about implementing your idea.

You need to find resources, usually money or capital. You will probably need other people to help you or work for you. Take each segment of this process and go after it. Don't let negative naysayers make you quit. The founder of the Pizza Hut franchise was told by a prominent business man that "nobody will want to buy this" and refused to invest in the start-up of the Pizza Hut business. He later referred to that as one of his missed opportunities.

3. **Share your vision.**

Nobody succeeds in life by themselves. Jesus sent the disciples out two-by-two. Solomon wrote in Ecclesiastes 4:9-10, "Two are better than one, because they have a good reward for their labor. For if they fall, one will lift up his companion." We all need someone to help us when we are discouraged or down. Share your goals and plan with someone who will be an encourager to you. Sometimes family members are not the best people to do this, but often they are. Sam Walton started Wal-Mart, but his brother, Bud, was by his side helping him.

Be careful about telling too many people or doing too much bragging about what you are going to do. When we do too much talking and not much doing, we will get a reputation for being heavy on the talk but light on the action. People respect action, not talk.

4. **Reward yourself upon completion of your goal for a given project.**

When you set out to do a project, reward yourself when you reach certain milestones on that project. After you have worked very hard for a long time, take a vacation. For eight years when I was developing our campground, I worked very long days, seven days a week, from May into September. By September I was worn out, so we took some time off and went on a vacation. The greatest reward that a person receives by developing persistence is the satisfaction of knowing they have completed a task that they set out to do. A job well done will bring great personal satisfaction and happiness.

Another phase I used in my motivational talks was "Success by the yard is hard, but by the inch a cinch." To keep on going and not quit we need to continue to move forward a little at a time. Sometimes we give up because the task seems too big. Someone once asked, "How do you eat an elephant?" The answer: one bite at a time. Keep going. Don't quit. You will reach your goals.

Quotes:

"Success seems to be largely a matter of hanging on after others have let go." William Feather

"The difference between a successful person and others is not a lack of strength, or a lack of knowledge, but rather a lack of will." Vince Lombardi

"The man who has done his level best…is a success, even though the world may write him down a failure." B.C. Forbes

"Perseverance is failing nineteen times and succeeding the twentieth." Julie Andrews

"It's always too early to quit." Norman Vincent Peale

CHAPTER 9
GETTING EXCITED, STAYING EXCITED – DEVELOPING ENTHUSIASM

"When you wake up say three times "I feel Healthy, I feel Happy, I feel Terrific!"

When I was seventeen, I left my job with the florist to sell Fuller Brush door-to-door. Selling with Fuller Brush was strictly a commission job. If I sold brooms, mops, brushes, etc.,

I made money. If I didn't sell anything, I made nothing. Under this kind of pressure I learned quickly what it takes to sell.

One thing it takes to be a good sales person, and to succeed in life, is enthusiasm. If you are not excited about the product you are selling, your potential customer will not be excited. I learned quickly that enthusiasm was an essential ingredient to being a good sales person. As a result, I was successful in selling for the Fuller Brush Company and Southwestern Publishing Company while in college, and later in many other ventures. I believe everything we do in life involves some degree of salesmanship. Just to get a job you must sell yourself to an employer.

In his course, *Science of Success*, Napoleon Hill listed seven benefits of controlled enthusiasm:

1. Controlled enthusiasm steps up the vibrations of thought and alerts the imagination.
2. It gives a pleasing, convincing color to the tone of voice.
3. Enthusiasm takes the drudgery out of labor.
4. It adds to the attractiveness of your personality.
5. It inspires self-confidence.
6. It starts the wheels of the imagination turning.
7. It aids in the maintenance of sound health.

Enthusiasm is defined in the dictionary as "lively interest, ardent zeal." Certainly, we should have a very lively interest and zeal in all that we do. Solomon writes in Ecclesiastes 9:10, "Whatever your hand finds to do, do it with your might." Put you whole heart into it. Be enthusiastic!

How to generate enthusiasm:

1. **Life is Great.** Get a positive perspective of life. We ought to be enthusiastic about life. How sad it is that many

people are not enthusiastic about life. Sometimes you hear people say, "Life is a bummer," and they mean it! It doesn't have to be. Life is exciting and life is thrilling if you decide to make it such. Jesus said in John 10:10, "I have come that ye might have life and have it more abundantly," or more fully. God wants us to have a full and abundant life. If we are experiencing the abundant life which the Scriptures describe, we will be enthusiastic about life. Often I say to people, "Isn't it great to be alive?" and it is. We should thank God for our life. We should be enthusiastic about life.

1. **Work is Great.** We should be enthused about our work. If you are a student, going to school is your primary job. If you punch a clock every day at a factory, you should be enthusiastic about doing so. You might say, "You don't know what it is like to work where I work." I have worked jobs that were not fun, but I was enthusiastic to have a job and maintained zeal and energy in the job. One of the best ways to be noticed at a place of employment is to be enthusiastic. This can get you a better job almost quicker than anything else.

2. **Help Others.** To be happy in life we need to become enthusiastic about helping others. There is little in life that brings more joy than when we learn to live for others. I believe that the abundant life Jesus promised consists of living for God and for others. In I John 4:21 we are told, "He who loves God must love his brother also." Just helping a person in even a small way can make a big difference in our lives. Often we don't even realize how much it means when we say a kind word to someone, ask about their loved ones, or do a small kind deed for them.

In order to create enthusiasm we must first believe in what we are doing. Why do people get so excited about their favorite sports team? It's simple. They believe in that team –sometimes even when the team is not having a good season. How do we get excited about our faith? By knowing what we believe and believing what we know. If you are going to be a good salesman you need to believe in your product. As a teenage salesman for Fuller Brush, I believed I was selling brooms, mops and brushes that were better than what a person could buy in the store. When I owned and operated a residential home for troubled youth, I believed our home was the best place a boy who was in trouble with the law could come to in order to turn his life around.

Secondly, put your whole heart into what you are doing. Half hearted efforts usually produce poor results and almost no personal satisfaction. We feel good about our work when we put our total effort into it. This is a process that must be maintained day by day. When we put our whole heart into something, we get rid of distractions. In this day of smart phones, social media, and electronic gaming, it is very easy to be distracted. If you are putting your entire self into a project or effort, you will need to minimize distractions while you are engaged in the real task at hand.

Thirdly, to be enthusiastic, act enthusiastic. Many times when we begin a project, whether it is mowing grass, raking leaves or cleaning the gutters, we really don't feel that fired up about it. But you should act enthusiastic. Then, before long, you will become enthusiastic. When you finish you will feel good about what you accomplished. When I was selling Fuller Brush, a speaker at a training session told us that to be enthusiastic we needed to walk faster than normal to the doors. He stated that successful people generally walk 25% faster than average. When you walk faster you create enthusiasm. For many years my wife complained that I walked too fast!

Enthusiasm is contagious. It spreads rapidly. If you are enthusiastic about a given thing, before long others will become enthusiastic about that exact thing. Over my career, I have spoken for more than a thousand groups. Whether it was a sermon, a lesson taught at school, a sales seminar I was conducting or a political speech, I knew it was very important to be enthusiastic. I make a practice to get to an engagement early enough to meet as many people as possible one-on-one and get my enthusiasm going. By the time I get up to speak I can share with enthusiasm because I have some sense of who is in the audience. If you are a history teacher, your entire class will become enthusiastic about history if you act enthusiastic. I had a teacher in a high school history class who absolutely loved history. He loved telling the stories of important people in history. His enthusiasm for history became an important part of my thought processes. To this day, I love to read and study history.

Another way to create enthusiasm within yourself is to repeat short inspirational sayings. W. Clement Stone, who was a successful insurance business man and motivational author and speaker, taught a large crowd of business people in Chicago to begin their day by saying three times, "I feel healthy, I feel happy, I feel terrific!" I have used this exercise on hundreds of groups of young people over the years. It has an interesting impact on the group. By the third time they are saying it, they feel better and more enthused about their day.

Any job worth doing is worth becoming enthusiastic about. Learn to get excited and to stay excited.

Quotes:

"Flaming enthusiasm, backed up by horse sense and persistence, is the quality that most frequently makes for success."
Dale Carnegie

"Success isn't a result of spontaneous combustion. You must set yourself on fire." Arnold H. Glasow

Chapter 10
Friendships Matter

No one in life succeeds by themselves. All of us need others. Anyone who accomplishes something great in business has others who helped make it happen. Look closely at the great entrepreneurs of the world and you will find close involvement of a second or third person. Friendships matter in life and in our journey of making a difference.

A definition of friendship that I have used for years in talks on the subject came from a pastor in Indiana who defined a friend as "one who influences in the right direction." In Proverbs 25:17 Solomon writes, "Iron sharpeneth iron; so a man sharpeneth the countenance of his friend." If someone is influencing you in the wrong direction, trying to get you to do that which is wrong, then he is not a friend at all. For ten years when I owned and operated the boys' home, I would interview each of the boys as they arrived. I would ask them what they did to make the judge put them into the system and send them to us. Almost without exception, they would relate a story of how they were hanging out with some "friends" and their friends convinced them to participate in an activity that was illegal. Very few ever admitted to getting into trouble by themselves.

Everyone wants friends. We like for people to like us. Part of being successful often means, in many people's minds, having a number of good friends. Friendships need to be developed. Whether it is in business, at church, even with family, developing true friendships takes work and effort.

How to develop true friendships:

1. **Be more concerned with being a friend than with having a friend.**

   Too many times we want friends because we want people to like us. This should not be our major concern. Our major concern is that we be a friend to someone else. We can be someone else's friend even if he does not consider us as his friend. We should focus on the needs of others and how we can be helpful to them, not on what we might get out of the relationship. For years, serving as a state legislator in Kansas, there were many times people wanted to be my friend because of what they could get out of the relationship. We elected officials were equally guilty. But I often took on causes and helped people specifically because I knew they would not be able to do anything for me in return. As a result, I was blessed with some genuine friendships that enriched my life. Others, who I thought were friends, came under the category of Psalms 41:9 where King David wrote "Yea, mine own familiar friend, in whom I trusted, which did eat of my bread, hath lifted up his heel against me."

2. **Be friendly to others – take the initiative in speaking with them.**

How often are we afraid to be the first one to say "Hello," or "How are you?" Be the first to greet a new person that you have not met before. Proverbs 18:24 says, "A man that hath friends must show himself friendly." Take the initiative in talking with others and getting to know them. Introduce yourself. Give them your name and ask them for their names. If you are like me, names are hard to remember. Use their name a number of times in that first encounter. When you leave their presence, write their name on a card or a piece of paper. In business settings, you can exchange cards. Find out things about this person, their family, their job, their hobbies, whatever seems right to ask under the circumstances. Be friendly to others and before long you will develop some good quality friendships.

3. **Learn to do sacrificial things for others.**
   You will probably recognize throughout this book that I consider real success in life to be helping other people. In developing friendships, we need to do sacrificial things for others. They need not to be large things. Even small things, little things, are appreciated by others. My wife and I got to know a couple who ran an antique store. We purchased a number of items at the store. They were certainly an interesting couple, so we invited them to have dinner with us at our home. I will never forget their comment. In their twenty-five years in business they had never been invited to a customer's home for dinner. We often have people in our home for dinner, so to us it wasn't that big a deal. We enjoy company. To them it meant a great deal.

   A poem, written by Charles D. Meigs, copyright 1907.

Lord, help me live from day to day
In such a self-forgetful way,
That even when I kneel to pray
My prayer shall be for others.
Others, Lord, yes others,
Let this my motto be,
Help me to live for others
That I may live like thee.
Help me in all the work I do
To ever be sincere and true,
And know that all I'd do for you
Must needs to be done for others.
Let self be crucified and slain
And buried deep; and all in vain
May efforts be to rise again
Unless to live for others.

4. **Be loyal to your friends.**

    If you have a friend, stick up for him or her. Be loyal. Be faithful. There are few things more heartbreaking than disloyalty. Loyalty means you believe and think the best concerning your friend regardless of the circumstances. If you were thrown in jail, whom would you call with your one phone call? What friend could you count on? When a teenager gets a car for the first time they often find they have a number of new friends. Let that car go away and see where those friends are. A businessman or woman who is prospering and doing well often has many friends. Let them go broke and have their business fail and they'll find out how many real friends they have. In politics when you win an election, you have friends everywhere. When you lose, your phone quits ringing.

    The Bible says, "A friend loveth at all times." This means

regardless of the circumstances, you love and are faithful to your friends.

5. **Keep Confidences.**

   This is closely related to the idea of being loyal to your friends. It is very important that you learn to keep the confidences of your friends. If they share something that is personal and ask you not to tell anyone, then keep your mouth shut and don't tell anyone.

   Proverbs 11:13 says, "A talebearer reveals secrets; but he that is of a faithful spirit conceals the matter." This concept led to some interesting situations when I was running our boys' home. When something bad happened (we found drugs, cigarettes, etc.) we wanted to find out who brought them into the facility. We would try and get the boys to tell us, since usually many guys knew. These boys were loyal to each other, not to us. It was at this point we would try and teach the lesson that you are not being a friend when you help someone do wrong. Even the law recognizes that you are partly responsible for a crime if you knew about it and did not report it.

6. **Be sure your closest friends share your values.**

   Hundreds of times I taught the phrase, "We become like those we are around." We talk like them, think like them, and before long, act like them. If you associate with caring people, you will become a caring person. It is hard to be influenced in the right direction if you are spending a lot of time with people going in the opposite direction. That is why people who have had trouble with abuse of alcohol must often find a new set of friends if they are going to quit drinking. Their friends at the local bar won't be much help to them in quitting the habit of abusing alcohol. We need to go places, such as a local church, and find friends who will influence us in the right direction.

Good friendship will make a world of difference in our success in life. Start today to develop new positive friendships in your life.

Quotes:

"Seek the counsel of people who will tell you the truth about yourself, even if it hurts you to hear it. Mere commendations will not bring the improvement you need." Unknown.

CHAPTER 11

MANAGING MONEY

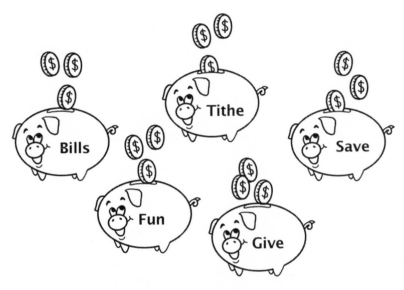

"Discipline the use of your money."

Having money does not equate to success. Mother Teresa did not have money but she was successful in helping thousands of the poorest of the poor. Under most circumstances, if you have no money, your opportunities are very limited. Some people claim the Bible says that money is the root of all evil. That is not so. First Timothy 6:10 says the **"love** of money is the root of all evil." (Emphasis mine.) When we become obsessed with having things and money we will become very miserable, no matter how much we have.

Money is no more than a tool we use to exchange our services for the services of another person. In some societies, and even in the past history of our country, people would use the barter system instead of money. Someone who sewed clothes did sewing for someone who gave them eggs and milk. In my first pastorate, my salary was quite small but the people were very kind in giving us meat and other farm products.

In order to maintain a successful life, it is vitally important that we learn to manage our money. It doesn't matter how much you make, if you constantly spend more than you make on a regular basis, you will go broke. A recent study showed that 70% of divorces are caused by money issues.

If a person can learn to manage money at a young age, then that area of character development will enable them to accomplish a great deal throughout their life. I believe that God cannot trust many Christians with large amounts of money simply because it would ruin them. Studies have shown that over half the people who win large lottery prizes are bankrupt five years later. Sudden wealth, and often inherited wealth, can cause great heartache. We are much more careful with money we have earned because we know how hard we worked for it.

Money Management Principles:

1. **Have the right attitude toward money.**
   We should look at money as a means of carrying out our daily lives. We need to eat, have clothes, shelter, and usually a means of transportation. But money itself is not the end all, be all, of life. Many very wealthy people

are miserable because their lives have been a process of thinking about themselves and accumulating wealth for themselves. Money enables us to provide for our basic needs, it provides freedom of choice in life, and enables us to do good things for others.

When we talk about meeting our needs, we need to define the term. How big a home do we really *need*? How nice a car do we *need* to drive? Each one of us must define those things for ourselves.

Money provides us the freedom to make choices in life. If you go into a Wal-Mart and have no money, credit card, check or any means of paying for purchases, you cannot choose to buy any of the thousands of items they have in their store. If you have $100 in your pocket, you can choose dozens of items.

I believe that having money gives you the opportunity to do things for others. Whether it is family, friends, or people you never knew, helping others is a key to genuine success in life. The more you earn and have, the more you can help others.

2. **Learn to be happy with what you have.**

The Apostle Paul wrote from a Roman prison in Philippians 4:1, "Not that I speak in respect of want: for I have learned, in whatsoever state I am, in this to be content." He goes on to say in verse 12, "I know both how to be abased, and I know how to abound; everywhere and in all things I am instructed both to be full and to be hungry, both to abound and to suffer need." In other words, Paul is saying no matter if he was broke or had a lot he was going to be content. He could be happy eating steak or just bean soup. Our happiness should never be determined by our outward circumstances. We can be happy if we have little.

Some of the happiest people I know are people who may be very poor by the world's standards but very rich in their faith and in their love of others.

3. **Learn to be a giver.**

To have the right attitude about money, we need to learn to be a giver. First we should give to God. The Bible teaches that ten percent of what we earn belongs to God. Some people think that when they have "enough" money they will give to the Lord what they should. It doesn't work that way. If you don't give to God when you have little, you won't be a giver when you have much.

We also need to learn to give to others. The more God blesses us, the more we should bless others. This helps a great deal with our keeping a right perspective about money because we realize how blessed we are when we see others with so little.

4. **Avoid debt.**

In today's society it is easy to borrow money. One of the first things students learn when they go to college is how easy it is to borrow. Credit card companies send many offers for offers for credit cards. College loans are easily available that require no payment until graduation. Easy borrowing eventually has a day of reckoning. The bills come due, the interest mounts up, and all of a sudden you can't pay what you owe. More than a trillion dollars is owed on college loans and many people's financial freedom is very limited because of their college loans.

One of the problems with debt is that you are always playing from behind. In a ball game, no team likes to play catch-up. Every team would rather have the lead. When a person is in debt, he is always playing catch-up. He is always playing from behind. The best way to get ahead financially and to effectively manage your money is to avoid debt as much as possible.

"Don't be imprisoned by a lack of self-discipline. Good discipline actually frees you to do great things."

5. **Develop a yearly financial plan.**

An earlier chapter discussed the importance of setting goals in life. That principle applies to financial planning. Each year you should set forth a financial plan for the year. How much do you expect to earn? What will be your expected expenses? Do those numbers add up? Are your expected expenses less than your expected income? Be sure to add an "unforeseen" category to the expense side since there are always things that come up that we did not foresee. Break those goals down into monthly segments. Then keep track of your goals. It is easy to have a spread-sheet on your computer that can tell you whether your income is keeping up with expectations and whether your spending is not exceeding what you thought it would. When you see those numbers getting out of kilter you can then make necessary adjustment. Adjustments are pretty simple when your numbers don't add up. Either you increase your income or reduce your expenses. By keeping track on a monthly basis you will be able to make necessary adjustments before you are in financial trouble.

6. **Learn to Save Regularly.**

Our lives are a series of habits. One important habit we should all develop is the habit of saving money. When you spend everything you make and you have no reserve on hand, you get in trouble quickly when an unexpected emergency comes up. One Christian financial expert suggests that we give 10 percent of our income to God and 10 percent to ourselves in savings, then live on the rest. Remember we all adjust our life- styles to the level of income we have. Unfortunately, some people elevate their life-style with the use of credit, which ends up causing real problems.

When saving money, be sure to keep the money in a separate account where it is not too easy to get to. A jar in your bedroom usually doesn't work since you have very easy access. You might have one account for emergencies and then a longer term account for longer term goals. Dave Ramsey is a Christian financial expert who offers tremendous information on this subject. He shows people how to live debt-free and develop a great financial plan for their lives.

Having money saved offers a number of important advantages. It enables you to handle emergencies without having to borrow money. It enables you to take advantage of opportunities that may come along that require quick money. Most business opportunities require that we have some of our own money to put in up front. When you have cash in savings you can take that extra trip or vacation that you may have dreamed about.

"Plan the use of your money – save a little of every dollar you get"

Managing your money well is vital to your real success in life. If you want the freedom to live well and help other people you need resources to do it.

Quotes:

"The habit of saving money requires more force of character than most people have developed for the reason that saving means self-denial and sacrifice of amusements and pleasures in scores of different ways." Napoleon Hill

CHAPTER 12

TURNING PROBLEMS INTO OPPORTUNITIES

**"Some problems don't seem good at the time but
eventually help us grow and become stronger"**

Everyone has problems. There isn't a person on the face
of this earth that doesn't face some kind of a challenge.
Problems fall into two basic categories. First, we all have personal
challenges. These include financial, health issues, family conflicts,
or even emotional issues. You may need to lose some weight. That
is no easy task. You may not get along with some family members.

It may be hard for you to make friends. All of these things come in the personal category.

"Sometimes things we don't like are the best things for us"

The second category of problems would be business or professional issues. Things we face at work or school. Our job may be very challenging. Getting along with our boss or co-workers may be difficult.

No matter which category your problem falls into, you need to think of it as a good thing and develop a positive mental attitude about it. Every problem you have can be turned into a great benefit.

The Apostle Paul speaks to this issue in I Corinthians 10:13 when he states, "No temptation has seized you except what is common to man. And God is faithful; he will not let you be tempted beyond what you can bear. But when you are tempted, he will also provide a way out so you can stand up under it."

The word "temptation" here means trial, testing, or problem. He starts out by saying that we are not the only person ever to experience the issue we are facing. Sometimes we all feel like "nobody has ever gone through what I am going through." Not true. We are not alone in our suffering or time of stress. Many people are having the same experiences you are going through.

Then Paul declares, "God is faithful. He will not let you to be tempted beyond what you can bear." You may have heard the phrase, "If God brings you to it, He'll bring you through it." It's true! There are lessons to be learned through every trial. If you are struggling with money, God is teaching you how to manage it. If you are looking for work but cannot seem to find a job, God may want to teach you how to create your own job. I never worried about being unemployed. I knew there was always something I could find to do to make some money, even if it meant cleaning people's yards or garages.

Paul concludes this verse by telling us that when we do face life's challenges, God will provide a way for us to be able to handle it. We need to pray. We must seek other people's counsel. We must read God's Word. Through various means, God will show us a way. You will find new strength to move on and overcome your problems.

So why do we have to suffer through problems in the first place? If God wants us to be happy, why aren't our lives easier? These are complicated questions with complicated answers.

We are a lot like raw metal and God is a lot like a blacksmith. In order to clean and shape the metal to perform its intended purpose, the blacksmith must hold the metal in the fire until it gives up resistance and allows itself to be molded and shaped. You are a piece of raw metal that must be molded and shaped into what God wants you to be. It takes fire, or trials and tribulations, to do that. My first child died after living 18 hours. At the time I was a pastor of a church and thought this is the most horrible thing that could happen to a person. I asked God why and didn't seem to get an answer. As life progressed, I was blessed with four healthy children, but I also had a special empathy for people who lost children. God is shaping you and me through every trial, temptation, and tribulation through which we suffer. He is teaching us to be like His Son, Jesus Christ, and we will be rewarded with greater character and much success.

Turn Your Problems into Success:

1. **Ask God for wisdom.** It is important to seek divine guidance when it comes to the problems in your life. In James 1:5, James tells us, "If anyone of you lacks wisdom,

he should ask God, who gives generously to all without finding fault, and it will be given him." (NIV) Talk to God about the issues you are facing.

2. **Define your problem as precisely as possible.** Writing it out will help you to make it clearer. Do you understand what you just wrote? If you are depressed or sad and unsure why, try to be specific and pinpoint exactly what is making you unhappy. If you are short on money, are you spending too much or earning too little to meet your basic needs?

3. **After you define your problem, say, "That's good!"** Remember, if you keep a positive mental attitude, you will be able to deal with your challenges much more easily. We often get into a negative thought pattern when we think of the issues we face. Reverse your thinking process and begin to think positively about what you face. Say to yourself, "I will find a good answer to this issue. I can do it." When you get a positive frame of reference, you will be able to come up with creative solutions to your problems.

4. **Make a list of all the benefits that can come from your problem.** Once you begin thinking positively about your problem, start thinking about what you can gain from it. You can grow in your character, improve your relationships with others, increase your faith, or learn a new skill. Pretty soon you start to realize there's no challenge you face that you can't find some benefit from.

5. **List possible solutions.** Now it's time to start brainstorming for solutions. Brainstorming is putting down every idea that comes to you or those with whom you are working regardless of how wild it may seem. No negativity is allowed in good brainstorming. After you

have the list, go back and begin to evaluate which ideas have merit and which ones don't. If you are short on money, which is a common problem for many people, you must increase your income or cut your spending. Whether it is personal, your business or a government unit, there are never enough funds to do all you want to do. We brainstorm on how to cut expenses. We brainstorm on how to increase our income. Write out the possible solutions and then select the best ones and move forward.

6. **Determine when a problem must be dealt with.** I have, over the years, taken an issue I face and tried to determine when I needed to make a decision. If I faced a large tax payment, I knew when I had to send the check in so I would allow different ideas to simmer in the back of my mind as to how I was going to make that payment. I did not allow myself to worry, fret, or become anxious about the challenge, I just let it simmer on the back burner and then the day I had to make the decision, I pulled the trigger and did what I had to do. By doing this, often solutions come along that you had not thought of before. Plus you sleep a lot better. I like this phrase, "Don't worry your worries before you need to." Sometimes problems solve themselves.

7. **Take action.** Do something. Doing nothing will usually make your problems much worse. You will never overcome a challenge by sitting around and doing nothing. If you are trying to lose weight in order to improve your health, you need to do some things. Get the fattening foods out of your house. Start exercising on a regular basis. Find someone to be accountable to in your process of weight reduction. Remember, we don't usually succeed without someone else helping us. Look

at your list of possible solutions to whatever issue you face and then act on each one.

There will never be a time in your life when you will be problem free. Once you realize that, you can deal with problems as they come along. You will find that you are meeting your challenges with positive energy instead of allowing yourself to get drug down in negativity. This will lead you to great success and accomplishment in life.

Quotes:

"We can't solve problems by using the same kind of thinking we used when we created them." Albert Einstein

"The ultimate measure of a man is not where he stands in moments of comfort and convenience, but where he stands at times of challenge and controversy." Martin Luther King, Jr.

"Every problem has a gift for you in its hands." Richard Bach

"The measure of success is not whether you have a tough problem to deal with, but whether it is the same problem you had last year." John Foster Dulles

CHAPTER 13
FAILURE-THE STEPPING STONE TO SUCCESS

A person's ability to succeed is directly related to his willingness to fail. No one succeeds at everything they try every time. In fact, most successful people have experienced more failures than they did successes. Babe Ruth held the home run record in baseball for decades. Most people don't realize that when setting those records he also had the most strike-outs. When we become afraid of failure it results in our not trying. Many churches, businesses, and individuals get caught in the sea of mediocrity because they are unwilling to take risks for fear of failing.

One reason we fear failure is because of concern that if we flop at something, we will be rejected by our friends, laughed at by our family, or thoughtless of by our co-workers. The opposite is true. Most people respect those who try and fail a great deal more than those who never try at all.

In 1990, I bought the church campground in Goddard, Kansas. After about five years of hosting family reunions, camps, retreats and running an RV park operation, I found my stride and was doing fairly well. I then became aware of another church campground for sale about an hour and a half away. I thought if I could do it at one place, why not two. I purchased the other campground and began developing it. After two years and considerable investment, I discovered that I was no good at being in two places at one time. I did not have a good second level of management at either location. I decided to sell the second camp and concentrate on the campground where I lived. I failed at running two campgrounds at once but I learned an important lesson about developing good management below me. The rest of the story about the second campground is that about two years after I sold it, oil was discovered on the property and the new owners are doing quite well!

We can learn valuable lessons from failure. Many businesses fail because of poor management of the company's money. If you discover you don't manage money well, find someone who can help you. The second year I owned the campground, I was audited by the IRS. Since I did all my own accounting, I had to try and show them all the details of my operation. It wasn't that large and I hadn't earned a profit yet but it was a challenge showing that to them since my bookkeeping was so poor. I quickly hired someone else to do my bookkeeping and taxes and to this day let others handle things for me when it comes to accounting. I learned from my failure. Failure can be a positive force in our lives if we take the lessons learned and apply them to our next project or venture.

Failure can strengthen our character. Our character is what we are on the inside. It is what we are when no one is looking. It is what keeps us going when we want to quit and give up. Abraham Lincoln lost most of his elections before he was elected president. He served one term in Congress and then lost an election to the Senate. But he did not quit. He stayed by his beliefs and eventually became the president who saved our nation from being shattered into pieces. Thomas Edison is known for his many inventions which make our lives better today. What most people don't remember is that before each of his successful inventions he had hundreds of failed attempts.

Nobody wins them all. No salesman sells everyone. Jesus Christ did not win over every person to whom He talked. Everyone loses sometimes. The people who come out on top are those who can lose but then get up and try again. It doesn't matter if you fail 19 times, just so you get up the 20th time.

Failure is not fun, but a person will never attain any great heights of success unless he is willing to first accept the fact that he may fail. Then when you do fail, pick yourself up and go at it again. Determine to learn from your mistakes. Determine that the next time you will win.

Quotes:

"Success is how high you bounce when you hit bottom." George S. Patton

"Success is falling nine times and getting up ten." Jon Bon Jovi

"The successful man will profit from his mistakes and try again in a different way." Dale Carnegie

"Success is not final, failure is not fatal; it is the courage to continue that counts." Winston Churchill

"I've failed over and over and over again in my life and that is why I succeed." Michael Jordan

"Develop success from failures. Discouragement and failure are two of the surest stepping stones to success." Dale Carnegie

"We fall forward to succeed." Mary Kay Ash

CHAPTER 14
USING TIME WELL

**"Time is life. Give someone some of your time
and you have given them a piece of your life."**

O ne thing everyone in the entire world has the same
amount of is time. Each of us has 24 hours in our

day, 60 minutes in each hour. How much a person gets done is determined by how we use those hours and days.

Let me ask a question. What is time? The best definition of time I have heard is that time is life. When you give someone your time you are giving them a part of your life. You can never get it back. If you give someone money, you can get more money elsewhere. When you give someone your time, it cannot be regained or replaced. When we realize that time is life, then we recognize that when we are wasting time we are wasting lives. In the Bible we are commanded to "redeem the time because the days are evil." Certainly God wants us to use our time wisely. People who are putting together the success puzzle have learned to use their time well. They have learned how to balance the many demands each of us have on our time.

Managing your time:

1. **Time is precious.** Many young people think they have all the time in the world. They think because they are young, they have many years to accomplish things. As we age, we begin to realize how quickly time passes us by. When we reach retirement age, we wonder where all the years have gone. No one has a guarantee on life. We really don't know how long we will live. We may live only another year. Wouldn't it be tragic if you wasted the last year of your life? Time is the most precious commodity we have. Learn to squeeze every ounce of usefulness you can from every minute of your time.

2. **Plan the use of your time.** Set up a schedule. Some people think that a schedule will make them a slave. Just the opposite – it sets you free! When you operate by a schedule, when you plan your work, when you set aside

certain times to study, read, and do the things you ought to do, it frees you to do those things you really want to do.

Often the use of our time is determined by others. Someone comes by and suggests that we do something that does not fit our schedule. It may be something you should do such as helping a neighbor in crisis. Schedules are important but so is flexibility. Pastors find it challenging at times to keep a strict schedule because people don't go into the hospital when we have time nor do they die when it is convenient for us. But if distraction is not a good idea, having a schedule will help you let others know that their idea doesn't fit your schedule for that day. You need a plan for each day and then work that plan. Plan your heaviest work for when you are the freshest. Don't wait until you are tired to take on the most difficult task you had planned for the day.

3. **Learn to concentrate.** For most people it is important to think of just one thing at a time. Keeping our mind on what we are doing helps us to use our time more wisely. It also helps us to finish tasks. A lot of us have convinced ourselves that we can multi-task, doing a number of things at the same time. Most of the time that is not as productive as we think. Texting while driving a car is not a great idea. Concentrate on the road. Your family will be glad to have you back home alive and oncoming drivers will be grateful to get to their destination safely.

4. **Take a break.** If you are studying hard for a final exam, take a break after an hour or two. Ten minutes or so will help your mind relax and make it more efficient when you resume your study. If you are doing strenuous physical work, take a break after a couple of hours and let your

body and mind relax for 15 minutes. You will get more work done in the next couple of hours than you would have otherwise. A person cannot work effectively if he is weary and tense.

5. **Do not be a perfectionist.** There is a difference between striving for excellence and being a perfectionist. The first is obtainable, gratifying and healthy. The second is just the opposite. It is unobtainable, frustrating, and even can be neurotic. It is a great waste of time. When you do a job, do it the best that you can. If you can honestly look yourself in the mirror and say that you have done the best that you could in the time you had, then be happy about it and realize you have used your time well. You can waste a lot of time when you try to be a perfectionist.

6. **Learn to say no.** No one can do everything that people want them to do. Students need to choose between various activities in school and church. Adults with families are constantly challenged by the demands on their time by family members, their jobs, civic responsibilities, and the things they enjoy. Sometimes we just need to say no. Learn to decline, tactfully but firmly, requests for your time that do not contribute to your overall goals. People will respect you for declining to join a board or take on another responsibility more than they will if you accept the position but then do not fulfill your responsibilities. A schedule will help you to explain why you can't take on something someone is asking you to do.

7. **Learn to do it now.** We can help ourselves a great deal if we develop the habit of doing it now instead of putting off until tomorrow what we should do today. Life has many deadlines. The IRS wants your tax return by April 15. It is easy to put that off. If we just sit down and do

it or get the information to our accountant now instead of waiting until later, we will feel better and not get in trouble with the IRS. This principle is very important with little things. Little things can quickly pile up and become big problems. It is easier to clean up our mess from one meal than it is to wait until we have dishes from four meals. We always feel better when something is finished. When it is still hanging out there after days of being on our mind, it becomes a bigger issue than it needs to be. Do it now!

"Time runs by quickly. Use every minute wisely"

8. **Get others to help you.** This is called delegation. No one can do everything. I was the youngest of eight. We had a lot of dishes after each meal and no dishwasher. My mother made it clear that we kids were the dish washers – and dryers. She delegated house-hold chores to each of us and no matter how hard we tried, we did not get out of them. If you have worthy goals for which you are striving, other people might be willing to help you.

9. **Look out for time wasters.** There are many things that can rob you of valuable hours and minutes of your time. Video games, Face Book, texting, sleeping more than needed, TV, are just a few of the things that can become significant time wasters. None of these things are of themselves wrong, it is just when they soak up our time and keep us from reaching the real goals we have for our lives, that they can become time wasters.

Life is too short to waste a lot of time doing non productive things. Management of our time requires that we balance our different needs, desires and responsibilities. Going on vacation is not a waste of time. It is vital to your ability to be effective when you are working. It is important to your family. For the last 12 years we have owned a second home on Beaver Lake in Arkansas. Some may say we wasted time there. I disagree. It is a very valuable place where we refresh our bodies and mind and where we develop priceless memories with our children and grandchildren. One of our grandchildren, when he was less than two years old and was just learning to talk, said as he approached the lake house with his folks, "Papa's fun house!"

Since success in life really involves positive relationships with family and friends, having time at the "fun house" was, and is always, considered an important use of my time.

Chapter 15

Readers are Leaders

"Love reading – it expands your mind and your horizons."

The late W. Clement Stone said, "You are what you will be five years from now except for the people you are with and the books you read." We've already discussed the importance of developing true friendships and having friends that influence you in the right direction. I want to discuss the importance of developing the habit of reading. Readers are leaders.

Reading is one of the best means of gathering new knowledge, information, and inspiration. Through reading you learn the thoughts of others and gain the knowledge that may have taken them a lifetime of experience to acquire. When you read you learn to think, absorb ideas, and expand your imagination.

Our culture today offers a real challenge to reading books. One of the obstacles to learning to love reading today is the explosion of the electronic world. Video games have captured the minds of both youth and adults. People spend hours on end trying to blow people up, drive race cars, play sports, or doing dozens of other feats on a video game. Since games can be played on so many devices, almost everyone is exposed to these opportunities. Many of these games are fun and are not harmful but it is important that you exercise your mind with words. There are many good word games that can help build your communication skills.

The second challenge in our culture to reading is the television. When I was growing up there were three channels on TV. Our choices of shows were very limited and we did not spend that much time watching TV. Today most homes have access to hundreds of channels with unlimited choices of things to watch. For just a few dollars a month, NetFlix can bring literally thousands of movies and shows into your home. I believe that it is okay to have a TV in our home. We do, my wife and I enjoy certain shows, and I like watching the news. But TV watching can make us mentally lazy. When I don't feel like thinking hard on things and just want to relax, I will turn on a movie and enjoy the time. My mind does not have to work at watching it. If we are going to achieve a higher than average level of success, we need to exercise our minds by reading. One thing parents might do in handling the challenge of video games and TV versus reading is to allow a certain amount of time watching TV or playing video games for an equal amount of time reading. Even a 3-to-1 split, three hours of TV or Video games to one hour of reading would be a tremendous improvement over what I see with most children today.

One of the positive things about the explosion in technology is the development of ereaders where you can buy books electronically for a fraction of the cost of a regular book. You can also carry dozens or even hundreds of books on that reader which would not be possible with conventional books. These books can be uploaded to our phone, our computer, iPads, ereaders and other devices. This should encourage more reading by more people.

Once you realize the importance of reading you need to think through what you read. Remember from the chapter on developing a positive mental attitude, what we put into our mind becomes a permanent part of our subconscious mind and influences what we do and say. Some reading, such as novels, is for entertainment purposes. That is not bad, but to advance ourselves in reaching our goals we need to read things that will have a positive, motivating effect on our lives. It is important to read the Bible some every day. This is important to our spiritual growth. We should read material that will increase our knowledge of the field in which we work. How many of us would want to go to a doctor who did not read and keep up on the latest developments in medicine?

I was challenged at an early age to read biographies of famous people. I enjoy history, especially the colonial period of our country's history. I grew up in New Jersey near Philadelphia where there are many buildings and places important to the founding of our country. In the past few years, I decided to read the biographies of as many of our founding fathers as I could. It was very interesting to get the perspective of each founder on the events that took place at that time in the development of our nation.

It is a good practice to read the daily newspaper. A recent study showed that 60 percent of the people who read a daily newspaper were happier than those who did not. Again, you can read the paper on the internet, often for free. Reading the newspaper keeps you connected with what is going on in the world and in your own area. You feel more a part of your community and might be motivated to get involved and help make your community a better place to live. It also helps you to converse intelligently with your friends and neighbors. It informs you of new things that are taking place that may affect your life, either in a positive or negative manor. You may want to know when your taxes are going up and why. If there is a breakthrough in medicine that might help you, you want to know about it.

Finally, it is good to read inspirational and motivational material. We all get down at times. It is easy to get in a rut. Reading stories of people who have overcome major problems in life to accomplish great things will help us realize that we can do it as well. Anything from a Christian daily devotional to a motivational book can make a positive impact on your work and success in life.

I conclude this chapter with a list of books you might want to consider that will help you better yourself and become more effective in reaching your goals in life. All of these books can be found on Amazon.com or purchased at your local bookstore.

Inspiration 365 Days A Year by Zig Ziglar (Simple Truths)

Be the Leader You Were Meant To Be by Leroy Eims (Victor Books)

Life is Tremendous by Charles E. Jones (Tyndale House)

The Success System That Never Fails by W. Clement Stone (Prentice Hall)

Success Through A Positive Mental Attitude by Napoleon Hill and W. Clement Stone (Pocket Books)

Strength and Beauty by Dr. Jack Hyles (Hyles-Anderson)

CHAPTER 16
SUCCEEDING IN THE SEASONS OF LIFE

"Each season is different as are the seasons of life."

In Psalms 1:3 David writes about the blessed person saying, "He shall be like a tree planted by the rivers of water, that brings forth its fruit in its season." Solomon writes in Ecclesiastes 3:1, "To everything there is a season, a time for every purpose under heaven." A tree that is planted is a tree that is put somewhere for a purpose. In Kansas, trees were planted to mark property lines and to provide windbreaks for the open prairie. Each of us has been put on this earth for a reason. We should bring forth fruit–useful service–in each season of our life.

Life consists of a number of seasons, such as our youth, early adulthood, middle age, and our senior years. Each of these seasons presents different opportunities and different challenges. Each season of life involves a different definition of success. As a young person, your greatest challenge is to get the best education possible and prepare yourself for what you hope to do with your life. Early adulthood usually involves the development of a career and the raising of your family. The goals we have for this stage in life will be different than those we will have for our senior years. Middle age often involves our children leaving home and our being at the peak of our earning capacity. Life sometimes becomes a little easier during this season. Our senior years present a different set of opportunities and challenges, depending on how well we have prepared for them.

How to be successful in each season of life:

1. **Recognize the season of life you are in.** We need to acknowledge where we are in life and set our perspective accordingly. If we are raising our children, then accept that as the most important thing you have to do with your life at that time. If you are starting a business, accept that the startup years will be much more difficult than the time when the business is running well and is firmly established. When I was a teenager I always wanted to be a little older than I was. I wanted to do the next thing I had planned for my life but couldn't because I wasn't old enough. In New Jersey you had to be 17 to drive a car.

For years I couldn't wait to be old enough to drive. Too many people are trying to live in a season of life that has not yet come their way or are trying to look back and be something they were in an earlier season but can't because of their age.

2. **Recognize various factors may alter your season in life.** How and when we move from one season of life to another may vary according to circumstances beyond our control. Health issues may cause us to have limitations on our activities we did not expect at our age. Family circumstances may alter your season of life. Many people today find that after they raised their own children, because of unfortunate situations they must now raise their grandchildren. Since people are living so much longer, it is common for someone to reach retirement and find they now have a parent living with them. That may limit their freedom to do some of the things they planned to do during retirement.

3. **Accept the season you are in and determine your goals accordingly.** I believe God has a purpose for our life every day we are living. It should be our goal to discover that purpose and then fulfill it to the best of our ability. It may call for us to modify some of our plans to fulfill His plan. We should always remember that fulfilling God's purposes in our life is the source of real happiness and fulfillment. That is real success.

4. **Be flexible in adjusting to the changes in life that come with the various seasons.** Most of us do not like to change things. Most men, including me, do not want their wives to put their favorite easy chair in a different location in the room. Some of us don't care if she ever moves any of the furniture. Changing jobs can be a challenge at times.

Moving to a new area of the country can cause stress. Change in life is inevitable. Things will never be exactly as they were ten or twenty years ago. People change. People die. If you live long enough, you discover that many of the people you were close to are no longer around. We need to be flexible and develop new relationships that will enrich our lives.

5. **Always be looking to the future not living on the memories of the past.** If you want to be really alive, vital and vibrant in life, you must be always learning and growing. We should never stop learning. This involves reading, listening and being involved with new people and new ideas all the time. No matter what season you find yourself in, if you stop learning you have stopped living. In our society today, there is no excuse for not continuing to learn. The internet and modern technology infinitely expand the limits of the information available to us. We just need to reach out and grab it.

The most important thing I hope you take away from this chapter is that God has a special purpose for your life regardless of what stage you are in. I believe we can be useful to Him and others until the day we die. In fact I believe God takes us from this world when He no longer has a need for us to be here. He doesn't keep us here to take up space. He wants to use us to be helpful in blessing others and accomplishing his objectives for this world. Determine to take your current season of life and live it to the fullest for His glory.

CHAPTER 17

PSALM 1 – GOD'S PROMISE OF PROSPERITY

I n Psalms chapter one, God gives us an outline of how to prosper in life. David begins in verse one by saying, "Blessed is the man." The word blessed means to be happy and joyful, or complete in life. God wants His people to be blessed. Some people think the more miserable we are the more spiritual we are. I disagree. In verse three of this chapter the writer goes on to say about the blessed man, "whatsoever he doeth shall prosper." God wants to prosper us. That prosperity may involve different things for different people. I do not suggest that it is God's purpose to make every person rich. Wealth can actually be destructive to some people and God knows who these people are.

The Psalmist first lists three things that the blessed man does not do. Remember, being successful in life involves doing a number of positive things but it also entails not doing certain things.

First, we are told the blessed man, the happy person, does not walk in the counsel of the ungodly. This means we don't listen to and take advice from godless people. We may not be able to control who we work with but we can control who we spent our free time with and who we listen to for advice. Remember, we become like those we are around. If you listen to people who have no room for God in their life, before long you will not think the spiritual part of your life is important either.

Second, the blessed man will not stand in the way of sinners. This means you do not do the things sinful people do. I'm not going to make a list of what I believe are acceptable and unacceptable behaviors of the Christian life. Each of us has a different perspective on various activities. I do believe that the Spirit will make clear to us when we are engaging in activities that are contrary to positive spiritual development. We need to listen to the promptings of God's Spirit in our own life. We are never really happy when we know we are doing things that are wrong. Remember, the wages of sin are always paid. A Christian can not involve themselves in sinful practices and be truly happy and blessed.

Third, David says the happy, blessed man does not "sit in the seat of the scornful." A scornful person is one who makes fun of spiritual things. People who use God's name in vain and make fun of spiritual things are not the kind of people with whom we should spend time. They will not lift us up, only tear us down. You will not remain serious about God and the things of the Lord if you spend a lot of time with people who scorn or mock spiritual things.

David then goes on in Psalms 1 and tells us positive things the blessed and happy man does.

First, we see in verse 2 that the blessed man "delights in the Law of the Lord." This phrase is referring to the Word of God, the Bible. Throughout the Bible, God reveals himself to us and reveals His plan for our lives. We are told how to have eternal life through Jesus Christ. The blessed man is one who delights in God's truths as they are applied to his life. We should read the Bible on a daily basis.

Second, we are told in this verse to "meditate day and night" in His Word. To meditate means to think on or ponder. When you read or hear an idea or thought from the Bible, let it swirl around in your mind. Think about it. Talk with someone else about it. Let it grow and mature in your mind. Many times, we do not absorb a new thought or idea the first time we are confronted with it. That is why you can read a passage of Scripture two dozen times and the twenty-fifth time you get a new perspective about it.

Third, we are told in verse 3 to be "like a tree that is planted by the rivers of water, that brings forth its fruit in its season." I dealt with this verse in the last chapter but one idea I want to add is that fruit is born over time. You do not plant a fruit tree and the next month start picking fruit from it. Some trees must grow a number of years before you get fruit from them. An olive tree must grow for seven or eight years before you start picking olives from it. But then you can get fruit for the next 100 or more years. We can't rush the seasons of life, nor should we. God usually has a time of preparation before He can use us to accomplish something significant for Him. Moses spent 40 years on the back side of the desert before God used him to lead the children of Israel.

Also we see in this verse that we are planted by "the rivers of water" which means we are put somewhere that we can receive nourishment and strength on a continual basis. The blessed man continually receives strength, wisdom and encouragement if we stay planted by God's source of strength.

Finally in verse 3, we are assured that "whatever he does shall prosper." Some people tie this verse to only financial prosperity. It is true that if we follow God's ageless principles for success in life we will generally experience financial prosperity. But it is not limited to that concept. Many people lead a significant life of service to God but are equally as happy and blessed as the person who may have wealth. The question is, are we fulfilling His goals and purposes for our life? That's what will make us truly happy and blessed.

The rest of Psalms 1 contrasts the ungodly person, and how they will not receive God's blessing, with the godly person from the first three verses. The ungodly person will be "like the chaff which the wind drives away." Chaff is that part of the wheat stalk which has no value. When wheat is processed, the chaff is blown away to reveal the kernel with which we make flour.

David concludes this short chapter by assuring us that "the Lord knows the way of the righteous but the way of the ungodly shall perish."

Determine to be one of God's blessed, happy people. Follow His principles in life as set forth in His word, the Bible.

CHAPTER 18
JOSEPH – LIVING GOD'S SUCCESS PRINCIPLES

One of my favorite stories in the Bible is that of Joseph in the Old Testament. Joseph was the next to youngest son of Jacob, who had 12 sons. He is one who applied God's principles of success from the time he was a young man until he died. I have taught this story dozens of times in our residential boys' home. Joseph illustrates many of the principles that are taught in this book. Let's look at the four primary seasons of Joseph's life: the dreamer, the slave, the prisoner, and the second most powerful person in Egypt.

Joseph the Dreamer: As a youth of 17, and the son of Jacob's favorite wife Rachel, Joseph had a special place in his home and in his father's heart. In fact, today we would call him the spoiled son, or Dad's favorite. Jacob even went so far as to make a special coat for his son. It was a coat of many colors and set Joseph apart as someone special. His brothers resented his relationship with their father and Scripture says they hated him.

Joseph had a dream. Dreams in that time had special

significance. Jacob, Joseph's father, had a dream in Genesis 28 where God revealed to him that he would have a special place in God's plan for his chosen people. Joseph's dream was that there were sheaves (stalks) of grain in the field. The sheaves stood up and his brothers' sheaves bowed down to his sheaf. He then later had a similar dream involving the sun, moon and stars with the same theme that the brothers would bow down to him.

Needless to say, when Joseph shared this dream with his brothers, it did not go over too well. In fact, the brothers hated him even more. There is no emotion more harmful than hatred. It has caused the downfall of many people. It will rob you of your happiness and joy and even destroy your health. Joseph's brothers were tormented for many years by their hatred of their brother.

Jacob responded to his son's dream by rebuking him. He "kept the matter in his mind." He knew dreams often meant something but he did not want to see the turmoil that was taking place in his family. Joseph was referred to as the dreamer. When he was sent by his father to check on his brothers and they saw him in the distance, they declared, "Behold, the dreamer cometh." They recognized his coat from a good distance.

Being a dreamer is a good thing. Most of the great things done over the last two hundred years were accomplished by people who had a dream. The founding fathers of our country had a dream of a free, independent, prosperous country and sacrificed greatly to achieve that dream for our benefit. Joseph's dream instilled within him that God had a special purpose for his life. He knew he was here for a reason. Successful people have a sense of God's purpose for their life and dream of what God can do through them. They then take their dreams and put them into clear goals followed up with specific action to reach those goals.

Joseph the Slave: When Joseph's brothers saw him coming across the fields of Dothan, they conspired to kill him because of their hatred for him. Jesus equated hatred with murder! The oldest brother, Reuben, intervened and suggested they put him in a pit instead. His plan was to get Joseph out later. Then, while most of the brothers were eating, a caravan of Ishmaelites came along on their way to Egypt. The brothers, without Reuben present, decided to sell Joseph to the Ishmaelites, who in turn sold him for a profit in Egypt. Slavery was a common part of the culture at that time. Joseph went from being a favored son to a slave in one day.

When they arrived in Egypt, Joseph was sold to Potiphar, an officer of Pharaoh and captain of the guard. Joseph was to work in Potiphar's house. Joseph had to learn a new language, a new culture, new customs, and to eat different foods. We know that Joseph was both a slave and a prisoner for a total of 13 years. We do not know how long he was in each situation.

What we can assume about Joseph as a slave speaks very well of his character and what he learned as a youth. He apparently worked very hard, had a good attitude, was trustworthy, and had the best interest of his master at heart. Imagine having a positive attitude when you went from being a spoiled rich kid to a slave in a foreign country. He did it. His good work ethic and honesty enabled him to be promoted to be the head of all Potiphar's household. He was entrusted with everything it took to run the large operation. The other slaves worked for him.

After a number of years, Potiphar's wife became interested in Joseph in a romantic and immoral way. She tried to entice him a number of times and each time increased the pressure. Joseph believed that such behavior on his part would not only be a sin against his owner but a sin against God. Joseph kept his moral compass even when he was away from the influence of his father. His refusal to become involved with her culminated when she grabbed him and tried to force him to seduce her. He ran out of the house, but she had his cloak in her hands. When her husband came home, she accused Joseph of the very thing he refused to do. Often in life we are mistreated by others. People try to take advantage of us in one way or another. Regardless of the circumstances, we should do the right thing. Joseph did, and eventually God blessed him.

Joseph the Prisoner: Potiphar could have killed Joseph on the spot, but instead chose to have him put in Pharaoh's prison. I don't think he totally believed his wife, but he could not very well do nothing. In prison we see Joseph's character take him to the top again. After a while, he was put in charge of the other prisoners. Again, I believe he demonstrated a positive attitude, a good work ethic and a trustworthiness that caused the keeper of the prison to have utmost confidence in him. No matter what we do in life, we should demonstrate these qualities and they will carry us far. People need to know our word is golden and that we can be depended on to do what we say we will do. It does not matter whether we like our circumstances or not. Genesis 39:23 says, "The keeper of the prison did not look into anything that was under Joseph's authority, because the Lord was with him and whatever he did, the Lord made it prosper." God wants to do that for each of us.

While Joseph was in prison, Pharaoh became angry with his two officers, the chief butler and the chief baker. He put both of them in prison with Joseph. While there, they each had a dream, but they could not understand their dreams. They found out Joseph could tell them what their dreams meant. He did. One of them would be restored to his position with Pharaoh and the other would die. That is exactly what happened. The butler was restored to his job in the palace.

Joseph asked the butler to remember him when he stood before Pharaoh and to speak to Pharaoh on his behalf. He did not remember Joseph. Sometime later, Pharaoh had two dreams no one could interpret. The butler then remembered Joseph in prison and told Pharaoh about him. He shared how Joseph interpreted his dream and the dream of the baker. What Joseph said happened exactly as he said it would. Pharaoh then called for Joseph to come to him from prison and thus began the fourth season of Joseph's life.

Joseph, the second most powerful person in Egypt: After being cleaned up, shaven, and given some good clothes, Joseph stood in front of the most powerful person in the world at that time, Pharaoh. Pharaoh related his dreams to Joseph and Joseph gave the interpretation of the dreams. He told Pharaoh there would be seven years of great crops and then there would be seven years of extreme famine in Egypt and the rest of the world. He advised Pharaoh to appoint someone to oversee the gathering of food for the seven years of plenty so the people would have food during the seven years of famine. Pharaoh believed Joseph's interpretation of the dream and liked his idea of gathering food during the good years to cover the difficult years. He then appointed Joseph to be the overseer of the gathering of the food and also made him the second most powerful person in Egypt, second only to Pharaoh himself. In one day Joseph went from being a slave to prime minister! I like to imagine what Potiphar told his wife when he went home that night!

In the journey of life, and in our effort to succeed, it is not uncommon for God to work in sudden ways. We can struggle with a project for a long time and then all of a sudden things break loose and good things happen. The tough times are what make us able to handle the good times. There is a reason why people who win large lottery jackpots often have their lives destroyed. They did not struggle to earn that money and thus do not know how to handle the sudden influx of wealth. When you work hard at something for a long time, you appreciate what it took to get where you are.

Joseph led Egypt in the gathering of food for seven years. Then when the famine hit he was in charge of distributing the food when people tried to buy it. His family in Canaan was experiencing the same famine and after a couple of years ran out of food. Jacob sent ten of his sons to Egypt to buy grain. When they arrived in Egypt, guess who they had to stand before to ask to buy food? You guessed it, Joseph. They did not recognize Joseph because it had been 22 years since they had seen him. He went from being a 17 year-old youth to being almost 40. He had a beard and spoke the Egyptian language. When they came before Joseph to buy grain, they didn't recognize him. This is where the real challenge began.

To be successful in life, we need to learn how to deal with people who wrong us. Joseph had great reason to be bitter and angry at his brothers. Now that he confronted them in person, he struggled with the issue of forgiveness. After a series of events taking place over a period of a year and a half, Joseph came to the point of being willing to forgive his brothers and restore their relationship. Joseph could now see God's plan for his life. In Genesis 50:19-20 he proclaims, "Do not be afraid, for am I in the place of God? But as for you, you meant evil against me, but God meant it for good, in order to bring it about as it is this day, to save many people alive."

It may take some time for us to understand what God is up to. If we take Him at his Word and apply the principles in the Bible to our lives, we will experience the joy and satisfaction of knowing we are living in His will. One of the keys to this is learning to forgive those who wrong us. It is not possible to get very far in life without people taking advantage of us or wronging us in some way. According to Scripture, we have no option but to forgive. By doing so we can move on and devote our energies to striving for the real dream God has given us for our lives.

Throughout his life, Joseph applied most of the puzzle pieces for success in his life. He had a vision that God was going to use and bless his life, a dream. He demonstrated a positive attitude under difficult circumstances. He worked hard whether as a slave, a prisoner, or as prime minister of all of Egypt. He certainly showed us how to turn problems into opportunities and he did not quit being faithful to his beliefs. What may have at times looked like failure to him, God helped him see as actually for his long-term benefit. His effective management of both time and money was revealed by how much responsibility he was given during each of the seasons of his life.